Sexy Mush

Additional copies may be ordered from the publisher
for educational, business,promotional or premium use.
For information, contact ALIVE Book Publishing at:
alivebookpublishing.com, or call (925) 837-7303.

ISBN
978-1-63132-085-9

Library of Congress Control Number: 2019920925
Library of Congress Cataloging-in-Publication Data
is available upon request.

First Edition

Published in the United States of America by ALIVE Book Publishing
and ALIVE Publishing Group, imprints of Advanced Publishing LLC
3200 A Danville Blvd., Suite 204, Alamo, California 94507
alivebookpublishing.com

PRINTED IN THE UNITED STATES OF AMERICA

10 9 8 7 6 5 4 3 2 1

Sexy Mush

L.H. Maloney

ABOOKS

Alive Book Publishing

The author ...

LH Maloney blends words that burrow in your heart deeply, finding comfort nestled in your soul. To take in his poetry is to go on a journey that you never want to end. He makes you want to go on and on, diving deeply into a universal vision all can see and feel yet no one can quite explain...unless they know you.

LH Maloney knows what wonders stir inside all of us about love, life and everything we experience, remember, and long for. With his words, he pulls your own feelings up and out for you to behold and languidly bathe yourself in the warmth of his soothing words. Unafraid to take you inside yourself, his vision is vast, his longing and desire to share with his readers the often-incomprehensible mirror of the heart and depths of the soul, so be prepared to read on and on. Come away with a feeling that refreshes and introduces you to your own heart and soul as you travel along with LH Maloney. Wholeheartedly his readers crave the feeling he evokes and urge "write on, LH", and now the gift has arrived. Gozar (Portuguese, "enjoy") as you dip into this premier 21st century wordsmith's wonderland. The going is easy on this journey. Come along!

Linda Hope

I believe in love and all of its complicated, messy consequences

... LH Maloney

CONTENTS

My love

Lying beside you tonight, watching you sleep
i hesitate to wake you, but
i really feel the urge, now,
to say thank you, again

from the day we met, my life has changed
that emptiness I used to carry in my heart
has been filled with the joy, you,
your love brings me each day

now, because of you,
i feel my life is complete,
with you, your love and support,
I am whole and able to love, and give love
the way you deserve, with all my heart

so I'll just whisper in the moonlight,
thank you, my love,
for every moment you spend with me
tonight, tomorrow, forever
i love you

what do you wish for?

what do you wish for?
is it soft and warm and quiet,
or
is it electric and cool and loud?

what do you wish for?
is it just out of reach,
or
is it already deep in your heart?

what do you wish for?
do you recognize it in the eyes of a stranger,
or
in a familiar, knowing touch?

what do you wish for?
when you find it, do you know,
before you let it go?

what do you wish for?
tell me...
what do you wish for?

Late afternoons

late afternoons,
it was her habit
to take me to her bedroom
there, carefully,
she removed my clothes
and my inhibitions

as the sun tore a jagged orange-pink rip
across the invisible gray sky
i reclined to enjoy her hunger
for all of me,
as passionately into the young night,
we consumed one another

when you are alone

when you are alone,
in your own quiet place,
the sole inhabitant of your solitude

close your eyes,
be still,
til your heartbeat is the only sound

then feel deep
inside
your essence

and touch again
innocence
your baby smile
your child's play
your yearnings
for first love
a real romance,
the purity
of sunlight
of fresh air
of new snow
of your joy

there
is
the only peace left

                                        in that place,
                                        in that peace

open your eyes
and you will
see me
do this,
and i will be there,

you will see me

                                        i will be there

Most of all

it would come as some surprise to you
to know when I enjoyed you
most of all
the time we shared
when I alone could know

the morning sunlight
scattered
translucent brown in your hair

the rise and fall of your chest
with rhythmic breaths
gentler than snowfall

and your sleeping softness
pressed head to toe
against the length of me

when I mapped your contours
memorizing your touch, sight, sound and fragrance
inch by languid inch

I enjoyed you sleeping most of all
because just to be there we loved one another
most of all

change in two

we can be
so afraid
feeling love

that

we cringe
at the very
thought of it

we can be
so brave
feeling love

that

we revel
at the very
thought of it

if only you knew

if... only you knew...
what i feel in your absence
you would know why...

i remain speechless
away from your radiance
in the shadow of unfilled desire

if... only you knew...
what i feel in your presence
you would smile...

for me
there would be perpetual
joy

if... only you knew...

unspoken

I flattered myself
with your attention,
your smile

but I just knew it was spread
only across my mind

then I realized, we share
this attraction, though

unlike our easy conversation
it remains unspoken

like a secret
you told me
that I told you

and no one else
ever knew

that my smile
is because of your smile

Bess Laments

in sultry air,

Gershwin plays,

Bess laments

enthralled,

i listen

and ponder,

why (?)

there is so much more beauty

in a world

that already has you!

love delights

love delights
in a simple touch
in things unheard, but felt

love delights
in the slightest smile
at the memory of a kiss

love delights
in weeping eyes
of lovers' good-byes

love delights
in a lonely lover's
longing

love delights
in two beating hearts,
at once, in tandem

love delights
in moonlit skies
with gleaming starry eyes

love delights
in the passion

of midnight romance

love delights
in the verdant green
and flowers of early spring

love delights
In the laughter of children
falling in the new grass

love delights
in the promise
only love can keep

that love delights
only love, delights

hunger

the hunger
in our eyes
is the longing

left by imagination
for the daydreams
and wishes
to come true

and feed our bodies
with the food

of each other

from before

are *you* the one?
the one who is supposed to
show me how to feel
love
again?

are you the one?
the one who i am
supposed to know
supposed to know
how to love
again?

are you the one?
who is supposed to know
who i am
supposed to love

are you the one?
don't i recognize you
from before?

today, tomorrow, forever

my love...
the day we met,
my life ended

my past slipped silently, suddenly
(imperceptibly) away

i was reborn

in the breath of your kiss,
nurtured in the radiance
of your smile,

and my entire future was foretold
in the joy of your laughter

today, tomorrow, forever,

i live...
by the grace of you

my love...

what mattered

today was an excellent day
the sun shone

                        but it didn't matter

the birds sang of spring

                        it did not matter

the children laughed at play

                        but it didn't matter

i looked out on a strangely quite world

                        it did not matter

violence had ceased

                        but it didn't matter

there came talk of peace too

                        it didn't matter

my work was done with ease

                        but it didn't matter

i saw you and what we shared

                        was all that mattered

to me

remember ...

hearing

a guitar string
shimmering with the last
vibrato from a touch,

seeing

a tear drop welling
in the eye of one
who had to say goodbye,

feeling

the icy tingle of snow blown
across your face,

or

the sight of the largest
moon you
ever beheld ...

life's summary
encapsulized

in memories of moments
that made you alive

remember ...

Encore

your fragrance lingers on my memory (so real)
your body pressed (so close) leaves a indelible impression
your movements melted into mine / mind

we danced
your embrace tightened
as i lost track of time
and all time became
that time   as

we danced
i followed as i led you...
around, around
never further than a whisper away
speechless, i filled your arms

we danced
the silence stopped our slow-motion swirl
a dream at conclusion,

we danced
...encore

it wasn't enough for you...

it wasn't enough for you

to touch me

you had to take me apart (easily)

your wave of love melted the sand levee

round my heart

your sensations picking my defenses apart

take this man, feet of clay -

just let me stay - close to you

it wasn't enough for you

to take my mind

your loving left me blind

through the shadows of unlove,

your beacon shone

your smile now lights my day

(i) can't fight you,
would never try to

because no force withstands the softness -

of being close to you

it wasn't enough for you

to touch me

you had to give me hope

lost love can live again

i'm of a mind to give again

with you loving me this way

take my care - and stay

just keep me - close to you

there is a way

there is a way
we love
that is spiritual
we touch the deep
dormant inside
of each other's soul
where God has made a special place
that He/She alone knows
how/when to fill,

there is a way
we love
that is emotional
from iceberg cool
to furnace heat
we range in and out
of composure, of rage, of exhilaration
and the solemn bless-ed peace
of our love

there is a way
we love
that is sensual
no other body
inflames this passion
no other touch moistens and delights

so far sweet
beyond words, beyond imagination,

and beyond
the intense tingling...

there is a way
we love
that is so private
we become lost in its intimacy
with tentative steps
we approach one another
from inside out,
believing
there is a way

what we feel

what we feel
together
and apart

bears the blended uniqueness
of our first child

a product
of our closeness and caring
for one another

we sacrifice
our solitude
our separate quiet

to partake

of the greatest pleasure
of the mightiest power
of the tenderest feeling

of sharing love

the sun is a thief

the sun is a thief...
he has a stolen
his brightness
from your smile

unknowingly,
he left
enough
to make me happier
than two lifetimes
of his shine

this season

in this season of hell,
i melt
with your name on my tongue,
i congeal.

once upon a time

once upon a time

the darkness of your eyes

contained a universe

in which i became

unexpectedly and gladly,

lost forever..

I did not care

I did not care
who could see that I wanted you
came to need you
and intended to have you
body and soul

and that the love we shared was so sweet
that we wore the delight
on our faces for anyone to see
how much we enjoyed each other's
minds and behinds

and no matter how odd it looked
it was obvious we enjoyed each other
 all that joy leftover from touching and loving
just proved we belonged together
and I did not care who could see

how much I cared

until whenever

never doubt

that there is a time for us

that only time divides us
from the nearness we crave,

that there always will be a tomorrow
waiting,
ripe and delicious,
for us to eagerly devour,
to savor,

that i will wait
until whenever
for you
to share my life

never doubt

that whenever comes

i know

whenever comes

NOT TODAY

the rain and cold
are seeping in
our plans will not work
there will be no beach,
not today

but there is hot chocolate
and we have quilts
covered with the words
of dreams we have spoken
that will warm us

and
i think
there is mix for brownies
we can make,
together

the rain and cold are out there
but inside
it is warm and alive

the weather is trying
to ruin this time of ours
together

but it can't
not today

in another time

we would have played
as children
lying head-to-head
in the grass
reading the clouds

in another time
you
were my prom date
sharing that first nervous sweet
long electric kiss

and not long after college
our wedding appears on the society page
(with icing on my nose!)

in another time
there would be sunny Saturday mornings
spent lazily lolling
in our big four poster bed
not long before the children
arrive to make us laugh
and cry

in another time
after children

after careers
come and go
i will pass away

smiling
asleep
in your arms

yet now,
in
another time
simply

i enjoy the warmth of your smile
the frolic of your humor,
the strength of your faith,
the joy of your living   and how

anxiously i await
your art
as yet unborn...

still,

longing for...

another time

The Reward

he reaches across the table
to brush her hair from her face

there, on the side of her forehead
an "L" shaped scar

a remnant of the childhood accident
which took her father

the scar,
the singular slight to her perfection

demurely, she drops her chin
and he takes her face into his hands

kissing the scar, he tells her it is beautiful,
this perfect imperfection

she looks into his eyes and
she smiles

thus, a wise man was rewarded
with the love of a beautiful woman

on either end

is it ironic
that on each end
of a spectrum
your feelings are
exactly the same

you care about nothing

on one end you bathe
in the giddy
invigorating invincibility
of emotional fulfillment

on the other end you drown
in the leaden
numbness
of empty heartedness

on either end
nothing matters
except

your love
or
your depression

isn't it ironic

only certain dreams

my hands,
my chest,
and my underarms
slathered with roll-on
i wander about aimlessly
nowadays, pondering
why fate does not always happen...

wondering
why a force
so strong as love
becomes lost
in an impenetrable mist
of yesterdays' "today,"
schedules, commitments,
and plain fear

i watched, and felt love
recede, time and again,
sucked away,
sadly,
i stood by
helplessly, hopelessly
dazed by fleeting moments
of passion,
of playful,

planful conversations...

and why
only some dreams
come true,
no matter
how hard
you wish,
you work,
you play,
you pray,
only certain dreams...

come true

it creeps

it creeps
upon you
s l o w l y

silent its arrival

doubt as you may your feelings

it sneaks
through the open window
of your mind

slipping
passed the veil
of your caring

straight
into your heart

within one blink
before your catch your breath
or even realize

you are in love
your only recourse...
enjoy the intruder

forever.

free fall

        Pray,
        for only God can stop your

free fall

        this flight was never planned
        why in your life would you ever
        want/need to fly again
        but now, you must

free fall

        who nudged you over the edge of reason,
        into rampant emotions
        did you will this,
        or were you willingly led to this

free fall

        time and space and thoughts
        all blur in a collage of feeling
        that you

free fall

        only God can stop you now
        but He doesn't / you don't want to
        cease this descent, too sweet, now

free fall

        when do you stop
        how far will you tumble
        does it always hurt so good,
        will you survive this

free fall

        hurtling through this seamless paradise,
        frightened,

you try to brake your

free fall

by clinging to love,
you brace yourself for impact
at the end of this dizzying

free fall

but continue your descent,
hopefully, dreaming you are not awake
and not in a

free fall

don't pray, don't fear, don't brace
just release, and

free fall

straight into my waiting arms
i'll catch you,
whenever you

free fall

Certain Arrival

through this window
i see the pavement below
that knows well
your approaching steps

and
mourns with me
your every departure

now

we both await
your certain arrival

and
even the morning air
is electric
with anticipation,
with the expectation,

and
for just one more brief
remarkable moment
filled with you,
your passing,
your certain arrival

and
its certain companion
joy

Never Near

Can you imagine

the incredible joy

i feel

when you are near me

i become frozen

in the unique, chilling

brilliance of your smile

your hot, star bright eyes

melt me in their gaze?

Can you imagine

how mundane

this world would be

if you were never

near me...

rollacoaster love

i *can* fly!

my face in to the wind,

arms outstretched,

i am joyous

i float carefree

in this delirious state

bound only by your love

lifting me, propelling me

violently to the summit

i'm above all of everything!

til the precipice appears

steep, and tingling

i drop

falling free

swerving, jolting

side to side

curving deep round

into the nadir of agony   i am

hurtling uncertain

into certain disaster

shaken back and forth,

forth and back

by your words of love and hate,

that love and hate   my heart

lodges in my throat

sure to burst
from the pain of the pressure
from the pressure of the pain
of your apathy

jerking me
to a stop   i come

to rest

thank you,

for bringing me back
down to earth

where is the end
of the line?

i want to ride again!

Carvão e giz abrigo
(a wet taste in the gaze)

i walk the street
like all the others
and
see them
hungry,
lonely,
a wet taste in their gaze

today, tomorrow,
forever
they search,
they hunger
from the insatiable
addiction,
to love
a wet taste in their gaze

for now
they meet eye to eye
willing to admit nothing
but they all know,
carry,
feel, and
recognize
a wet taste in the gaze

of each stranger
passing by
silent,
lonely,
hungry,
crying, alone knowing
today, tomorrow, forever
a wet taste in their gaze

[lust for the love for the feel of one another]

love come again

fast as some shadow
passes by
quicker than a wink
of your hazel brown eye
love once you came
and I let you in to play
but love don't visit here,
if you ain't gonna stay

be here till mornin' will ya?
spending just tonight?
up and gone, for some reason,
first light
best tune your music,
it's soundin' bittersweet
turn on your heels, walk,
quickstep away on those fancy dancin' feet

fast as some cloud, windblown,
floating high across my heart
leavin' this feeling
again, quite a bit, tossed
a little less of sanity
or just another lost day

love don't come again
if you ain't gonna stay

within your tears

within your tears
are worlds of feeling,

of delirious confusion
as you are submerged in love
again

of hurt you never
want to spread
beyond your heart

of hope you nurture
for life
as it should be

of desire so passionate
so consuming
your soul burns

and

of longing
for the comfort
of a life

again in order
and in love

they roll down
you cheek

rescued

by the subtle embrace

of my kiss

just when you thought it was safe

just when you thought it was safe

to disconnect your feelings,

he climbs the backstairs

of your mind

just when you felt it was safe

to unbind your heart's imagination,

he mails back the books he borrowed, with the note

"still thinking of us / loving you"

just when you realized how easy it was to go on,

he reappears

to melt your objectivity with the heat of his desires

and the embers of your passion

he still hasn't answered your questions,
"where he was, and why?"
"where he's been, since the last goodbye?"
you don't expect answers
so you never ask again

just when you felt you could let go

of the grip on yourself,

he is here

calling you out to play!

after your touch

the rest of the world
is harder,
because your gentle softness
lingers

though i frown,
the very thought of you
forces my lips apart
to smile

within my darkest corners,
your hope illuminates
against my will,
between my desires,
visiting with a companion,
that forgotten stranger
called happiness

after your touch,
a sunrise
am i too long blind to see...
the heat I feel assures me
you are here... still

i will and i will

and when
that very first kiss comes,
will its tingling electricity
be far behind?

and

how long will it be
before the earth spins in reverse,
the stars crowd into your eyes
to blind you

and

if it takes your breath away,
how will you ever get it back

and

stop dead in place
til you catch up

i will
and i will
stay for the whole delectable ordeal,

but

if,
and only
if,
you kiss me again!

and

kiss me again!

CAPTIVATION

no less stealthily
than a tiger stalks
does your liquid gaze
take captive my soul

no less savagely
than the tiger pounces,
does my heart race
at the vision of your smile

in this jungle world
so certainly
passions flare,
then flicker away

but ...

in the night of your hunt
still rages a flame
that burns unextinguished,
for the want of you

and never the captive heart
been so enthralled

your heart knows better

do you recollect those moments
so open and quiet,
yet so full
you can hear your heart
tell you
how right it is...

in those moments
when you find you
are doing everything
you want to...

like when
you are watching
the glowing sun set
and leaning softly
against the one you love
and neither of you care
if time just goes away
and has nothing more
to do with you
because

in those moments
time is meaningless anyway
your heart tells you

'forever'
and who are you
to disagree...

Pulling me close

now comes the time
deep in the night
i am alone   and
waiting
over the endless, hour filled minutes
to feel   you
through distance and space,
for yours is
the essential touch of love

undefined, unbound
beyond our comprehension
or reason
reaching and grasping
pulling me close,   and
back from any edge,
the undeniable touch of love

i know you are there...

even now... incandescent

hauntingly,

you

never leave me

along with the sun,

you

rise in my waking

thoughts, each day

behind me in the mirror

i see your dark eyes sparkle

making my way through the crowd

you

emerge before me

and with just a smile,

you

still ignite me

and i burn, even now ...

incandescent

for

you

If only you knew (redux)

if you only knew
how really close you feel
to the center of my heart

then
you would tell me more of passion
and other precious things
you would see the longing in my eyes,
that I know only for you
you would tread more slowly

and
you would handle all about you
with even a gentler touch

all because love changes

if only you knew...

daynight

today was a darkened eternity
without your face,
your voice,
your touch,
your glow,
in my life

though i persevered,
my reward
is darkness   again
as true night descends

when o when
will the sunshine
that sets
in the eyes
i love
light my daynight
and my way
to you   again

i miss you
and your light
in my daynight

Femme Fatale

when you feel
her presence

smoldering
as fires do
her heat intrudes
and your world ignites

your last conscious perception
greets her approach
sparkling eyes, above
the knowing seduction of a smile

opening with words you cannot hear
for you are forever lost
consumed alive within the burning
desire of flame

your passing will be mourned
the imminent cause of death...
femme fatale

forever will your memory
blaze with her sparkling eyes

Just Nothing

with nothing
to give one another
we found a way
and gave our all

we gave the sweetest gifts
of all, all of
our bodies and hearts
to one another

touches, secrets,
kisses, jokes, and smiles
that just didn't seem to fit
anywhere
else but
with one another

from nothing,
just nothing,
we gave our all

and there was nothing
anyone could see
that made us fit together

and with nothing to lose,

we made the most
pleasant satisfying love
that left us wanting
nothing
else but
one another

and
just nothing
else would do...

just nothing

You Entice Me

you entice me
with the soft wave of your hand
with gentle unexplored curves
with a knowing smile

i circle your flame
like a moth
and i burn for you

i am consumed
day after day
by your essence
your femininity

Burn

his voice was fire (simmering)

she burned to his songs

she drew near this fire

to test the warmth

laying with him in adoration,

to feel the heat

that fire she stole

and passed away

 to me,

so, now, i burn

not so much a theft

as a gift (transferred)

he smolders still

perhaps, hotter

for her touch

you may feel the stolen heat

in words, in sound, in song

now,

you burn...

Spring is

so much like your kiss
flower soft,
tingly electric,
warm, wet, sensuous,

stirring my blood

so much like your kiss
it comes alive
in my heart
and in my soul

it blossoms

so much like your kiss
it makes me warm
inside, all over

it delights

Spring is

so much like your kiss
that each time it comes,
reborn,
i fall in love

all over again

Leaving?

leaving me?

how silly to think you could ever leave!

distance is no obstacle

to a loving heart

or the foolish mind

that ever lets you

leave...

alone

Tomorrow

tomorrow?
you said tomorrow
tomorrow?

i can't make it
i'm certain

don't you know,
I die once
in the length of each day
without you

my tomorrow is a lifetime
away
small wonder this life of today
is so perfectly meaningless

without you

I must

time and again

just the memory of your closeness

blankets me,

comforts me,

touches and implores me,

nearer,

again and again

i come back,

as i must,

to you

half a rendezvous

sure,

i waited
at the appointed time and place
sitting, lap full of poetry books

between eBooks and tabloids
with screaming, annoying headlines
i waited

scanning pages of Mary Oliver,
Pablo Neruda, Sylvia Plath, Billy Collins,
and a torrent of anthologies,
all conducive to being deep
within one's self, and waiting

i waited
anxious to ask the security guard if he had noticed
someone of your description
though i have no idea how you appear today
but he is too busy, anyway,
policing the public restrooms

i waited
excited at the hopeful sight of your winter sweater
worn disappointingly by a shop girl doing inventory

who managed to deceive me long enough
to ignite more premature expectations

i waited
because i knew you would come
so each goose down coat rustling past
promised vainly,
to deliver the warmth of your smile

i waited
reclining in the plush
"sit and wait here in comfort" chair
lap piled with poetry brimming
with the love and living, and nature, and pain, and loss,
and joy and comic irony i'm feeling now

i waited
and always will because

it does not end here
and lasts longer than time
longer than i ever had you,

this love,
patiently is waiting

[i knew my parking space was too close]

why

if all the world
went away tomorrow
would i mourn

nothing
but the loss of you?

are you more
to me
than anyone?

are

>   your wits sharper,
>   your eyes brighter,
>   you more beautiful?

is

>   your touch lighter,
>   your voice more melodious,
>   your mind higher,
>   your kiss sweeter?

is

it because you care?

or

do i just think

i love you?

Once Upon a Different Time

once upon
a different time and place
our story will unfold
a romance, yes
but a drama and comedy
as well

you may not know it
yet,
though i perceive clearly
we will weather
every storm
and hold each other dearly

the author,
divine,
revealed it,
written in my heart,
eventually,
you'll feel it,
and realize your part

Help me out here

what shall i call this happy madness
all this unexpected joy?

my today became tomorrow
yesterday
as i felt all time implode

i've moved into the perpetual state
of gladness
living in your smile

how did I come to be so lost
deep inside what we have found

the newness, so familiar
in the excitement
of your kiss

is all the happy maddening joy
this lost and found heart can take
for now...

To where you start

don't be afraid
to meet up with destiny

there may be surprises,
pleasant surprises, like me!

you may search endlessly
all the while obeying what you believe
is God's plan

wary, but hopeful,
ever reaching out
with an open hand

deep, deep inside
far enough in
to touch your own soul
you may find the other half
to finally make you whole

time
and time
and time again
you return
to where you start

but there,
deep inside now
you will find my heart

Some time, now

I have been staring at this ten-year-old picture
of you for some time now,
black and white,
I have decided that I still love you
your absence and your silence
 notwithstanding, though
you never spoke of it much,
you just loved me fiercely,
genuinely, truly, quietly
the way a young body can
but that was then, and
there is the absence and the silence
to steal my fervor
but the memory of your genuine,
truly quiet fierceness is too strong

so, I have decided that I still love you,
and I probably always will

Heaven – on a rainy night

What did *you* see
as the raindrop shadows
danced across the bedroom walls?

I saw melting poka-dots
that dripped all over the bed,
and painted our faces
into Picassos of black and light

not especially memorable,
but you were there
in my arms
ignoring the rain,
the light, the dark,
the time, the future
everything,
everything except me

I thought that was the pinnacle of our romance,
and it was,

Heaven on a rainy night

So tightly

So many
sweltering Summer evenings
made so
not by descent of a sizzling sun
but the intimate heat
of our longing to be one

counting backward
from our children to come
it is now
that we surrender
to the mindless passion
that binds us
so tightly

regret

you can never imagine
how many of those stolen nights
i lay beside you
eyes wide open

in the creeping of the silent moon light
invading the picture window at the foot of your bed
filling each corner of the room, in turn
with the blue of night

how still i lay
in that light listening, and feeling
your breath rushing away
from our perfect moment

my young body
as close to heaven
as it could ever be on earth
and as far from any hurt
it is possible to know

there, resting,
across the naked landscape
of your skin
i regret
ever falling asleep

Parting

the last day
the last night,
with you,
the last hour
the last moment
the last kiss
the last hug
the last touch
the last glimpse
the last tear
the last thought,
in sweet sorrow,

is goodbye

Consummations

Late afternoons,
it was her habit
to take me to her bedroom
there, carefully,
she removed my clothes
and my inhibitions

as the sun tore a jagged orange-pink rip
across the invisible gray sky
i reclined to enjoy her hunger
for all of me,
as passionately into the young night,
we consumed one another

How old?

How old must I be?
that this song I know so well
is now disconnected from the lover I shared it with,
"our" song, we both swore - forever
 the song is still there
the song, the meaning, the feeling
still,
where were we then, and
who were you?

yes, I recall the smooth curve
of your young arching back,
melting into the soft valley of your thighs,
the trickling of our blended perspiration

how old must I be?
that distance and time transcend
that anxious love
how old must I be?

too old

Grace of the Wind

ever feel the wind
brush strong against your cheek?
invisible,
but discernibly
soft as a lover's caress

selecting you to kiss,
then hurrying away
to the cheek of another
so blessed,
by the grace of the wind

My tomorrow

the pleasure of your company
in our time together
has become the cool spring water
softly rippling over the rocks of my soul

and when i see you smile
the storm clouds, low over my day,
are broken
and your sun shines through

when you are with me
your closeness is comfort
that I have seldom known

and I am never startled
by your gentle touch

your eyes have taken me deep
and held me within
the softness of their gaze

and there
my hard times melt
into the comfort of you
beside me

when gone
i first realize the numbness
of the lack of you

and in all this feeling
i yearn to know
that you will be
in every tomorrow

Quarantine

I will welcome, if you will,

the madness of this affectionate, irresistible virus

we shall suffer

irreconcilably

from this fever of passion

alone together

we will bear

the textured heat

of an insatiable romance

in our quarantine of love

(and) no one else

I have always belonged to you
and no one else

before I realized
who you were,
you owned me,
and all that I am

became yours
when I realized
there was no one else
who knew who I was
in your embrace

even while I was careening
in and out of the arms of others
I belonged to you
I was unconsciously,
inescapably yours

no longer deaf
to the subtle sounds
of reality calling me
back to finish my life's work
of loving you

like no one else

The Only Sense

you intoxicate me so

so naturally

with a gentle beckoning

as irresistible as gravity

into your imaginary embrace

i fall

nearer,

the nearer you come

i suffer a head long tumble

provoked by your smile

balance isn't the only sense

i've lost

as you walk on by

you intoxicate me

fragrance and all

just passing -

bye!

left to share

we fell in love
there was passion enough to spare
fate tore us apart
with so much left to share

time dampened the memories
and fortunately, the pain
while the progression of life
and giving to others initially kept us sane

but the giving and giving
becomes a frightening drain
as does the wondering
if we could ever feel the same

when time takes its toll
must our love pay the price
or become just a memory
a convenient escape device

the questions, too many
the answers too few
my love though submerged
is steadfast, still true

i still want you to want me and i believe you still care

with unspoken longings
there is a missing lifetime of feelings
still left to share

Neruda taught

my love for you
is not a dark joy,
a thing inside of me

it *is* you
and I am whatever you are
whatever you become
I will be

if you love me
and carry me I your heart
there
we will always be

a fetish

her calves
were firm
and shapely

secretly
i would enjoy them
more than the rest of her
body

stroking them as we lay
intertwined, struggling
to grasp them
when we loved

feigning the conclusion of sleep
squinting though sunrays,
i would watch her move quietly
about the room on tiptoes
just exaggerating their shapeliness
their firm, young softness,
delicate, and strong

yearning to hold them,
squeeze them,
adore them
even when she was gone

Desejo de Amor *
 (Longing of Love)

desejo
the day of simmering heat
dissolves into the sultry
cool of evening

desejo
dark eyes meet my stare
fearlessly, then
never look away

desejo
the sway of samba
ends in tight embrace

desejo
close moments
shared in moonlight
end together in darkness

desejo
swallowed whole
in the mouth of a night
ravenous for passion

desejo
awakening, intertwined,

to tender touches and cafuné

desejo
for every kiss there is,
minus one
- the next

desejo
for a new day, and
the same, sweet conclusion

[*Dez-a-jay gee amore]

Two Views

my eyes fixed
on what is before me
in my view,
the nighttime road ahead
companioned more dearly
with the sight of you
your eyes
your smile
your naked skin

not here

on the empty road
within the darkness ahead
there is also clearly
your hand holding mine
your finger tips
traveling my body where you have already been
in the darkness

ahead

two views,
passing headlights
and you within my reach
always

filling the darkness

The Weight

the weight is too tremendous
the tons of time,
a crushing emptiness
that pushes down on me

since last i saw you

i feel my knees buckle
my back starts to bend
as i fall
to pray that i will not be mashed
beneath the seconds,
and the minutes,
and the hours,
and the days,
and the weeks,
and the months
and more
that wait is too much to bear

since last i saw you

Lovers Speak of Lovers Past

Lovers often speak of lovers past
with a romantic disappointment
their lovemaking
their attitude
their money
their conversation
their consideration
their communication
their dedication
their devotion
just wasn't right

lovers speak of lovers past
with a melancholy disillusionment
of those with whom they are through
that they speak of them at all,
says, once,
with all those faults
they were good enough
to love

It's time

the clock is s-ticking
how much longer
must I wait
as we draw nearer
enticed by fate

you know,
time's so slow
(imagine going forward in reverse)
no, it crawls ahead
and how can I feel worse?

I know it will come
the closer we get
I know it will be warm,
(just hope it's wet)

as we move even closer
I can only see your eyes
close them now
it's time
so, I'll act surprised
kiss me!!!

Touch me

touch me
with the softness of that light
shining in your eyes

touch me
with your hands that have only
accidentally held mine

touch me
with lips
whose warmth paints each smile

touch me
with a heart glow
that just melts mine

every once and a while
touch me

Blessing

sometimes
it is just as simple as your smile,
your handshake, or
just the inadvertent touch
of your hand

and later
deep in the day,
long after you've gone,
lingering, it is still there
fresh
not just in romantic musings
somehow your image is
all too real

this is the gift
of your memory
the light of your smile
the warmth your touch
each, to the soul
a blessing from you

and again

time and again
the memory of your closeness
beckons me,
surrounds me,
touches me,
implores me,
nearer
again
i must come back
to you. . .

Ever

I never forgot the comfort of your friendship
or the state of gentleness
in which you held me

and the love you gave
is an eternal pleasure
it is the sweet and lasting treasure
we shared

recounting now our nearness,
your sweetness has not diminished
and your flavor, as always, for me
the taste of memorable happiness

and the joy your introduced to my life, though peerless,
I vainly search for in every lover
and sadly, their perfection falls
grounded somewhere beneath your shadow

how foolish it was of me to say goodbye
and seriously believe that you could ever pass
from my life, my mind,
or my heart

the mind sees clearly
even with the closed eye

and you will always and illuminate my senses
even from the inside out

this is just to let you know
that your touch was always more than skin deep
and although your life may be too full to ever hold me
now, you are with me ever...

Dreamy Duet Mornings

Sing the song
you taught me
with love in every verse

let the lyrics
linger on my heart

let your music lift me
beyond space and mind

Sing the song
you taught me
With you and me inside

let the dancing take us
step into the glide

Sing the song
you taught me
reach deep into my soul

on dreamy duet mornings
our harmony unfolds

Too much time

your call was a smile!

your voice, a song

just the thought of you

once more,

is electric

my breath is shorter

my step quicker

my stride is longer

there is too much time

for me

before you

You deserve

in your life should be springtime, full
with all the colours of love

and summer, alive
with all the warmth of your heart

and sunshine aglow
with the brightness of your smile

and nighttime reflected
within the deep metallic shine in the darkness of your eyes

there should be a gentleness
worthy of mother and child

there must be softness
with the yielding vibrance of your touch

and love,
there must be love,
always love

Thank you for two

Two years!
you would think, my love
of an anniversary as a marking of a passage,
a passage of time,
yet more importantly, it marks what does not
pass or go, but stays

true love stays strong and grows even more intoxicating
ripening and fermenting with time
love that lasts spurs a hesitant, nascent hope
for two more years

so the time that passes leaving
behind what is stronger with age,
the articulate expression of our love

there has been fear and bad, but
so much more of the good,
feeling the joy and tenderness of love
grown deep, knowing, dependable

so look forward
and believe that with its passage,
time only enhances our love
true and strong

Apology from a friend ... a married lover

YOU
were delicious
and I was a
FOOL

whether you tempted me
with your sweetness or
i lured you with my eyes
then my lips,
we both devoured
FORBIDDEN FRUIT

I drank deep
we both reveled in the drunkenness of
TABOO

and the sinner's queasy exhilaration of
STOLEN PROPERTY

ENJOYED
with loved ones temporarily forgotten

we wallowed in our delirium
unconscious of
GUILT
until passion was extinguished

and rationales exhausted

naked bodies, naked souls
together   alone
apart from the ones who had our hearts

to whom we return hoping
forgiveness, never admitting our
SIN

committed
AGAINST LOVE
with a lover
who was married

to a friend

In your hands

sometimes in making ourselves
feel good
we make others feel good too
and when we make others feel good
life,
in that moment,
becomes very pleasant

but life is more than a single moment
and feeling good is habit forming
its better than feeling bad and
far better than not feeling at all

so everything you need
is in your hands
its just a question of where you put them,
and how well they move
when they get there!

It was more important

I look at the picture I took of you
that summer on the beach,
everyday

my memories of our closeness
are so vivid and, I guess, precious
but I also remember, I let you get away

once someone saw me staring at that picture
and asked, "did you love her?"
"yes," I answered thoughtfully,
"but at the wrong time, in the wrong way"

now
before me, stuck in my mirror's frame,
I just look at your picture
everyday

you know,
you were so near me, so often then
I wanted so much to reach and touch you, but
it was more important
to be your friend and amuse you

beside you in the sand
I could *hear* your eyes beckon me

within a welcoming gaze
but the simmering inches between us
was all the distance in the world to me

frozen in that moment and in the shadow of your smile
I caught you with my camera
and then lost you forever to a different time and place

now
I just look at that picture,
everyday
Only then

distance, and time
are not measured
by the heart

only the longing,
the feeling apart
in me   without you

feeling
not belonging
now,
and remembering a then
together

The question remains

I can never be lost
above all,

you

possess the power
to locate me,
ever certain of my position,
and condition
somehow you always know
where I'll be
right where you left me, yesterday ...

in love with you,
still ...

the question remains
will I ever be found
by you

I wrote you a letter

somewhere between, "hope you are well," and
"i love you,"
i mentioned the pure ecstatic pleasure
of your company
somewhere between, "how's the family," and
"i love you,"
i told you of the gentleness
with which you always hold me
and
i am certain i wrote of my feeling
at feeling your touch
and about your filling my longing for you
near me and
the simple beauty of any moment
with you in it

and somewhere between, "how's the weather," and
"i love you,"
i went on to say
that laying in your arms is a lingering dream
of a reality i want to share with you
again and again and...
how the next time, i will not leave that haven

between "i love you, "and "can't wait to hear back,"
was one unique and heartfelt letter

do you get it?

Lightly

Early morning lite

the sun's first rays

play peek-a-boo

with waking eyes

before the coffee steeps

or the time for eggs to crack

I watch you sleep

in the early morning

lightly

I touch your lips

with mine

Suonare

later in the day,

when the quiet sets in

i hear the music,

that I know is your voice, again

                                        o
                                      d
                                    n
                                  e
                                c
                              s
                            e
                          r
exclamations   c

utterances in a
                    l
                      t
                        o

whisper to me,

sotto voce,

let our symphony begin!

my demeanor

the outlook is more pleasant
far more than I could surmise
the view is simply lovely
when I gaze into your eyes

my demeanor is more optimistic
and spring is once again in the air,
I'm feeling a glimmer of hope again,
seeing its sunlight in your hair

the days are growing long
the heat sticks us all so fast
my curiosity is peaking
think i'll ever fall within your grasp?

the evening star is rising
and the darkness shrouds my view
my thoughts are turning,
as always, and ever, to you,
ever to you...

I love it, but I hate it

I loved being near you...
when we can be alone

I hate to know we cannot
remain just us

I love you getting close
without me asking, on your own
we must

in parting is sadness
we hesitate, but

I love your soft, well placed touches
your hand lingers

I hate it when you say,
"it's time for me to go"

I love your gentle kisses
With you playful tongue

I pray to stretch
each minute

I love your love around me
I was made to feel this way

let time slip by real s l o w
and in the end

I love the love we share
anytime of the day

I hate it when we finally say goodbye
a sad man, I turn and walk away

but
deep inside I cry
I hate to be without you
when I love to love you so

That night

after hours and passionate hours together all in a row
of what use is a tomorrow?
there is nothing life can bring me now as touching and fulfilling
as our last night together

who would need another day to live
if it would be anything less than that night
all there is left to experience now pales
after our night together

selecting a moment to be frozen in time
and living it forever and savoring it
for all eternity
that is my desire

after that night together
who needs tomorrow

the best part

ah,
to breathe again the air graced by your fragrance
like the first breath of life, invigorating

to see your glowing countenance, the glorious first sight
of a man born blind

to hear your song
voicing an echo to my lonely heart

to feel your touches on my body
is a soothing balm

all this to me is now the value of life
the best part

Tell her

my heart races
at the thought of you being
near

drums of passion
long stilled
by misfortune,
deception, hopelessness
are heard to beat again

or

could that be the sound
of just one heart
encouraged by the radiance of that
twinkle in your eye?

so too,

the succulent swirl
that curves your lips in a smile
beckons me to a world
where none may enter
without your willing leave

You appeared before me

once,
bewildered, but beautiful
you appeared before me

approaching,
I beheld your face and
its thinness
belayed the ethnic thickness of your curves

you spoke, and
the glow of the accompanying smile,
in your eyes, in your face
stole what was left of my sight

blind since that moment,
my vision grows
beyond me,
beyond you
all the way to my forever

there is no fantasy to the feelings
that circulate and
live and breathe
inside my inside and in time

I know that my sensation has overtaken you

what has infected my heart has touched yours
what always controls
when nothing stands in the way,
what never goes away,
what stays inside you
inside the deep, deep recess of your being
is love

it can live there and
it can blossom
it can grow
it can glow like it does
in your eyes,
in your smile

its just what I've felt, since first
you appeared before me,
for you

that first time
my arms encircle you
let me hold you
tight, tight enough
to convince you
to just relax against me

let me bear your weight
if for only   just that moment
just long enough

for you

to know the support and affection
you so deserve are here

for you

within my embrace feel,
feel enough
of what I have

for you

and know
as God has blessed us both
I am here

for you

Amaze

how
are you so happy
when there is so much
pain

how
do you float up above
the turmoil of the world
below

how
can you love so dearly
when no one is
worthy

I see you
contented, peaceful, loving
the way you are and you simply

amaze

Sometimes it is

sometimes it is enough
just to hold someone
in your arms
and know the pulsating closeness
of another,
beside your one

sometimes it is enough
to kiss
and feel that passion
can still dwell somewhere inside
your dormant senses

sometimes it is enough
to feel the love
you know you share

sometimes it is enough
to have your heart hold on
and on till
there is no more doubt
sometimes no time is enough

it just is

there is little more to say about love in bloom
except,
that it may begin uncertain,
but that is not insignificant

it grows, germinated by smiles,
soft whispers and welcome touches
it grows stronger and it holds firm
once nurtured, it cannot be destroyed
it just is
love is the emotion of knowing and sharing
in the heart, blossoming and thriving,
it grows more beautiful
as do lovers who share

let us then be as love
full of understanding the heart
and blossoming, growing stronger
and more beautiful

I wonder

who is she?
I wonder
this woman petite,
yet potently so,
with the innocent and
lovely smile of a little girl
yet eyes that smolder
within that feminine gaze

i wonder
does she know
in all of her existence
there is one so
intensely affected by it all
that he cannot speak,
i wonder,
who she really is

Lyrics from Limbo

in between the luscious, biting
grasp of your lips
and the furtive,
reluctant goodbyes

i live,

between the delicious daydreams
of last night's love
and the stark downer message
of your daytime decisions,

 i struggle,

between the sweet embrace of your thighs
and the resolution
that you are gone (or i am gone?)

i settle,

in between the joy of your voice
on the phone when i miss you so
and your begrudging, tentative admissions of love,

i nestle,

between the euphoric splendor of your very next real, deep kiss
and the nadir of darkness
where you alone can cast me

i float,

in an endless uncharted sea of Limbo
nurtured by your love
and cursed by your reason,

i need,

to escape because, i only know   i love you
and when awakened in my dreams
you really love me
too...

Into your eyes

when i look into your eyes

one million, million words
spill from my mind
and dibble in muddled puddles
at your feet

left speechless
just by your beauty
i stoop to scrape up the right words,
any words, to tell you...

that

when i look into your eyes
one million, million thoughts
race through my mind
they collide and numb my brain

left dazzled,
double-teamed by your beauty and my mind
i cannot even babble to you
how blessed i feel...

when i look into your eyes

ein ah petS

so what does this prove
this time
we are apart

how busy,
how distracted,
how mature,
how detached,
we are

i know i miss you,
i know you miss me,
i know i want you,
you know i want you,
yada-yada,

i want you near me now

and i know
no duty,
no job,
no church,
no child

can keep us apart ...
for long

yesterday, today, tomorrow

i taste
your last kiss
still

                   your flavor lingers on
                   my lips
                   in my mouth

i smell
your fragrance
when you're gone
still

                   i'm dizzy
                   from breathing
                   you in

i feel
your body
pressing mine
still

                   every contour of you
                   is a memory impressed
                   deep in every muscle, on my skin

i remember
your softness
in each caress
still

                   electricity jolts me
                   even now

                              with every touch
i imagine
your passion
in my embrace
still
                              our loving is magical
                              as we disappear into the land
                              of youandme
i know
your desire
it inflames me
still
                              ignite my being
                              so i can burn
                              for you alone
i want
you
near me
still
                              craving the indescribably
                              sweet joy of
                              loving you

yesterday, today, tomorrow

You are for me

there are times
when no food can extinguish
the ravenous hunger
i feel

it is for your body
for the taste of your flavour
the extravagant pleasure
between your milky thighs

my tongue is anxious
to do battle with yours
for the prize
of your mouth of your nipples
the palm of your hand
your tender syndactylies
the nape of your neck
and each ear lobe

now

i see you
in each darkness
where your curves caress
my empty yearnings
fulfilling my life,

and my dreams
of the heaven

you are for me

Caress

embrace me
and your fragrance lingers
long after,

my face, my chest, my arms
and my hands
bear your scent
and you
never leave me

i hold you still
and it is as though you still
embrace me

Touch

she mentioned that she slid her hand
under her man's shirt to massage his back
in a gesture of "it's alright."

"I felt the love, did he?"
without an answer, i flashed back

i pushed a cart through the wide market aisle
your arm looped mine
and we walked side by side, even closer

"i felt the love..."
before she could respond,
i continued,

'but you know, even better,
as i drove, she settled in the car seat,
turned toward me,
and
without looking, just touched me,
touched me with the lightest of touches
on the back of my neck

there, and then, an electric tingle,
that was the love

more than words, more than a feeling
"love is a touch," i said,
ask any baby!"

No night

the night
invented pillow talk
but did you know, it listens
and whispers back to lovers
the dreams that they share

the night
created passion
with barely audible moans
and sighs
with piercing screams
and giggles
that tickle the hardest
of hearts

the night
is full
of goodies
that no night
we share
should be without

eyes of one another

as the sun reclines

into the wanting caress of the sea

and the valiant moon

chooses to ascend

how vacant this beach

save you and me,

still nestled in our impressions

in the soft sand, and

lost within the eyes

of one another

Your Hold on Me

I noticed, as a child,
all the West Indian men of my family
would hug one another as a greeting
they were otherwise stoic
the practice was warm and sincere
and it made me happy to see
the hug took a special place within me
not casually given, received or noticed

a girl named VV stays on my mind
just because she took my hand
once on a walk,
I barely knew her

I love to cuddle.
is that a hug?
feels like it

all this leads me to you
our first hug was not casual,
it was forbidden
and as welcoming as an open door
into your life

it still has a tender meaning
holding memories of dancing in the dark,

showers together, and sleeping arm in arm

I never realized how much it all meant to me
until there was no more
I can't remember your last hug
which troubles me,
because I know you loved me then

much later,
a lady held me close,
leaned into my body
and held me tight around my waist
hers was a memorably eternal hug
and heartfelt,
but it couldn't measure up
to your hold on me

Getting Messy

I came
to play between her legs,
expecting less,
I did
that night

before
in prolonged conversation
about the minute alteration of her hair style,
or the perfection of a slightly overweight figure,
while sustaining eye contact
passed the point of innocent comfort
to advances beyond flirting

the prelude was the first kiss
in that fast food restaurant restroom
while changing for a jog,

and then the invitation
to an intimate supper at *her* place
an appetizer of petting,
snuggled on the living room carpet
an entrée of inevitable intercourse
a delicious desert of love

the offer of a warm wet cloth after

could not remove the scent,
the flavor, the taste of a woman
like a true soap shower

my clichéd departure,
hasten, half dressed,
through the bathroom window
was never part of my plan,
nor was the arrival of her husband

somethings have a way
of getting messy
even when you think you know
what you are doing
and with whom

Always the Same Dream

your dream,
always the same dream
the wet streets of Paris glisten
beneath the clicking of your quicksteps
as you pull your collar tighter
against the damp night
it's late
shop lights extinguish
around and above you
no matter,
two more flights and you are home
steps inside your door,
you mutate with the dusk,
within the cling of chemise,
into a create of comfort
momentarily resting lithe, languid
you find the silence
too imperfect and the throbbing emptiness
of your hands unbearable
stallion-like
your cello emerges
rosin, bow await
one instant of tuning later
you straddle its passive bulk
and begin the delicate foreplay of creation
soothing the longing of your fingers

on anxious trembling strings
moments pass
lost in your music
chin down,
eyes tight,
you nod and you sway
to the art of new rhythms
given birth inside
the tender smoothness of your thighs
it is then,
unannounced, unseen,
that he approaches
unknowing
and absorbed in your procreation
his presence eludes you
until his hands reach out
to cover your eyes,
startled yet
undaunted,
you play on
there is a need
and a frenzy
in your playing, and also,
he senses,
within your body
loins that straddle a wooden love
ache and long for his
girth between them,
his touch within them

dropping from your eyes
his hands journey
and fully cup your breasts
first lightly,
through fabric suddenly grown too thick,
with unnerving pressure,
he kneads there
nipples erect,
your perspiration beads a new
to match the moisture of his efforts
and the music must cease
as he deftly,
effortlessly
releases your buttons,
your inhibitions,
your desires,
one,
then another,
after another
his caresses
meet your naked skin
your heart now races
as you turn,
at last, to know him,
to see his face,
to give him welcome,
a new sun greets your eyes
and this dream,
as always

fades like the sleep
leaving you,
... unsatisfied

To die from love

In the Yin and Yang
of this world,
for each ecstasy above,
awaits an equal agony below

so when a love "to die for"
comes along
the journey just begins

an inevitable fall
from loves' embrace commences
a rapid descent within

far, very far beyond
the forlornness of depression
passed the anguish of melancholia,

to a private hell
constructed of deprivation,
devoid of the most vital nutrient,

a leech of life
just tantalizingly beyond
the describe grasp of death

many arrive,

surviving the fall, yet
none return

sadly, it takes too long,
you gave too much too escape,
your last worldly possession

the personal exquisite pain
you earned
lingering on, leaving you

to die from love

Sexy Mush

spilling out bodily fluids
in a collision of flesh
so sublime

pouring out lingering emotions
and cracking the hard rock of time

sucking the milk
of longing
and nurturing improbable dreams of love

foolishly clinging to a coming and leaving
made tender by the loss of your mind

and surrendering all your earnings
in a moment of promise
called touch me just one more time

surviving the dreams of tomorrow
dissolved in the present's reality gone sour

to finally, finally come to the realization
love is there, you'll need
sexy mush

born of emotion

it spills out uninvitedly

whenever there is love
whenever there is no love left
whenever there could be love or there was once a love

whenever the love you love is lost or
the love you love is found

whenever is the time, wherever is the place
however is the way
for having sexy mush

For more, visit

http://thepoetssight.com/category/poems

ABOOKS

ALIVE Book Publishing and ALIVE Publishing Group
are imprints of Advanced Publishing LLC,
3200 A Danville Blvd., Suite 204, Alamo, California 94507

Telephone: 925.837.7303
alivebookpublishing.com

www.ingramcontent.com/pod-product-compliance
Lightning Source LLC
Chambersburg PA
CBHW021101090426
42738CB00006B/450